The Golfer's
Little Instruction Book

Honor Books
Tulsa, Oklahoma

The Golfer's Little Instruction Book
ISBN 1-56292-606-3
Copyright © 1999 by Honor Books
P.O. Box 55388
Tulsa, Oklahoma 74155

Printed in the United States of America. All rights reserved under International Copyright Law. Contents and/or cover may not be reproduced in whole or in part in any form without the express written consent of the Publisher.

Introduction

Honor Books is proud to bring you *The Golfer's Little Instruction Book*, an inspirational and sometimes humorous compilation of wide-ranging quotations about the game of golf. It's sure to score a "hole-in-one" with golf fans, whether you just watch the game on TV or actually play a few rounds on your favorite links.

These powerful little insights will help you learn to stay out of "the rough" with classic advice from great golfers such as Tom Lehman, Scott Simpson, Arnold Palmer, Sam Snead, Jack Nicklaus, Lee Trevino, Chi Chi Rodriguez, Ben Hogan, and others too numerous to list.

Experts say the secret to a great golf game is a relaxed swing. So relax, take a deep breath, keep your eye on the ball, and start reading. We won't promise you'll shave any points off your game, but you're bound to win a few in the clubhouse when you start quoting *The Golfer's Little Instruction Book*.

4

The secret of golf is to turn
three shots into two.

Bobby Jones

Many times God speaks to us
through the things we love to do;
sports, hobbies, work, and
friendships. As a professional
golfer, I am often asked for tips
or advice. So here it is—listen
to what God can say to you
through the game of golf.

Tom Lehman

There is no such thing as a natural touch. Touch is something you create by hitting millions of golf balls.

Lee Trevino

While man's battle against himself
is undoubtedly at the heart of
golf's abiding appeal, the setting
in which it is played is for
most golfers, one of the most
wonderful things about it.

Herbert Warren Wind

Indeed, the highest pleasure
of golf may be that on the fairways
and far from all the pressures
of commerce and rationality,
we can feel immortal for a few hours.

Colman McCarthy

I'd like to think that my priorities are still my God, my family, and then golf. How I perform on the course does not affect my relationship with my God.

Tom Lehman

10

Nothing dissects a man in public
quite like golf.

Brent Musberger

There are no guarantees in
this game—not to mention
in this life—and we have
only a short time to enjoy it.
Even when I'm not playing
particularly well, I enjoy
what I do.

Scott Simpson

Talking to a golf ball won't do you
any good. Unless you do it while
your opponent is teeing off.

Bruce Lansky

As you walk down the fairway of
life you must smell the roses, for
you only get to play one round.

Ben Hogan

13

Golf is a game of days,
and I can beat anyone
on my day.

Fuzzy Zoeller

14

Real golfers don't miss
putts, they get robbed.

Unknown

15

16

I play with friends, but we don't
play friendly games.

Ben Hogan

The harder you work,
the luckier you get.

Gary Player

17

18

Victory is everything. You can spend
the money, but you can never
spend the memories.

Ken Venturi

Golf is 90 percent inspiration and
10 percent perspiration.

Johnny Miller

20

Most golfers prepare for disaster.
A good golfer prepares for success.

Bob Toski

There are three ways of
learning golf: by study, which is
the most wearisome; by imitation,
which is the most fallacious;
and by experience,
which is the most bitter.

Robert Browning

21

22

What other people may find in poetry
I find in the flight of a good drive.

Arnold Palmer

Always throw your clubs
ahead of you. That way you
don't have to waste energy
going back to pick them up.

Tommy Bolt

23

24

One of the most fascinating things
about golf is how it reflects the cycle
of life. No matter what you shoot—
the next day you have to go back to the
first tee and begin all over again and
make yourself into something.

Peter Jacobsen

Columbus went around the world in 1492. That isn't a lot of strokes when you consider the course.

Lee Trevino

25

Golf is the only game where the worst player
gets the best of it. They obtain more out of it
with regard to both exercise and enjoyment.
The good player gets worried
over the slightest mistake,
whereas the poor player makes
too many mistakes to worry over them.

David Lloyd George

Don't hurry, don't worry. . . .
Be sure to stop and smell
the flowers.

Walter Hagen

27

28

I realize that my gifts and abilities as
a professional golfer are directly from God.
I know that just as champions rise beyond
the mastery of skills to win in competition,
we can also use our gifts and abilities from
God to be champions in life.

Tom Lehman

When you reflect on the combination of characteristics that golf demands of those who would presume to play it, it is not surprising that golf has never had a truly great player who was not also a person of extraordinary character.

Frank D. "Sandy" Tatum Jr.

29

30

If you want to beat someone out on
the golf course, just get him mad.

Dave Williams

I probably have forgotten
more about golf than
I have ever learned.

Jack Nicklaus

31

There is one man who ought never appear on
a golfing green. And this is the good man.
Let him remain away.
That immaculate creature whose life is spent
in seeing his neighbour's faults and
comparing them with his own wonderful perfection,
is quite out of place amongst golfers.
They are all men, not saints.
Therefore let the Pharisee,
whose pretensions to superiority
we will never dispute, keep at home.

Dr. Proudfoot

Well, in plain old English,
I'm driving it bad, chipping it bad,
putting bad, and not scoring at all.
Other than that, and the fact that
I got up this morning,
I guess everything's okay.

Bob Wynn

33

34

It is nothing new or original to say
that golf is played one stroke at a time.
But it took me many years to realize it.

Bobby Jones

Practice puts . . . brains
in your muscles.

Sam Snead

35

36

In golf, as in life, it's the follow-through
that makes the difference.

Unknown

I've made a million, but
I don't have a million.

Walt Zambriski

37

Lay off for three weeks, and then
quit for good.

Sam Snead

No one who ever had lessons
would have a swing like mine.

Lee Trevino

39

40

Putting is like wisdom—partly
a natural gift and partly the
accumulation of experience.

Arnold Palmer

Eagles and birdies are more
often made with great putts
than with long drives or
spectacular iron shots.

Unknown

41

42

If you travel first class,
you think first class
and you are more likely
to play first class.

Ray Floyd

If you try to fight the course,
it will beat you.

Lou Graham

43

Real golfers don't cry when they
line up their fourth putt.

Unknown

I'm going to win so much
money this year, my caddie
will make the top twenty
money winner's list.

Lee Trevino

45

46

The greatest liar in the world is the
golfer who claims he plays the
game merely for exercise.

Tommy Bolt

Golf is a lot like business:
the more you invest in the game,
the richer you get.

Tom Tracey

47

48

Real golfers know how to
count over five; it's when
they have a bad hole.

Unknown

Faith has its share of bunkers, and
golf has its share of prayers.

Max Lucado

50

Half of golf is fun,
the other half is putting.

Peter Dobereiner

A ball will always come to rest
halfway down a hill, unless there
is sand or water at the bottom.

Henry Beard

51

52

It is impossible to outplay an opponent you can't outthink.

Lawson Little

Actually, the only time
I ever took out a one iron
was to kill a tarantula.
And I took a seven
to do that.

Jim Murray

53

54

I deny allegations by Bob Hope
that during my last game I hit an eagle,
a birdie, an elk, and a moose.

Gerald Ford

I've lost balls in every hazard
and on every course I've tried.
But when I lose a ball in the ball
washer, it's time to take stock.

Milton Gross

55

56

The reason the Road Hole is
the greatest par 4 in the world is
because it's a par 5!

Ben Crenshaw
(on the seventeenth hole at St. Andrews)

Man blames fate for other accidents but feels personally responsible for a hole in one.

Martha Beckman

57

58

Do I ever disagree with
him on course strategy?
NEVER . . . unless he's wrong.

Gary Nicklaus
(on caddying for his father, Jack Nicklaus)

You can talk to a fade but a
hook won't listen.

Lee Trevino

59

There is no movement in the swing
so difficult that it cannot be made
even more difficult by careful study
and diligent practice.

Thomas Mulligan

Golf puts a man's character
on the anvil and his richest
qualities—patience, poise,
restraint—to the flame.

Billy Casper

61

Everyone has his own choking level,
a level at which he fails to play
his normal golf. As you get more
experienced, your choking level rises.

Johnny Miller

Beyond the fact that it is a limitless arena for the full play of human nature, there is no sure accounting for golf's fascination. . . . Perhaps it is nothing more than the best game man has ever devised.

Herbert Warren Wind

63

64

All good players have good hands.
And I'm afraid
you have to be born with them.

Dave Stockton

When Jack Nicklaus plays well, he wins. When he plays badly, he finishes second. When he plays terribly, he finishes third.

Johnny Miller

65

Walter Hagen said that no one remembers who finished second. But they still ask me if I ever think about that putt I missed to win the 1970 Open at St. Andrews. I tell them that sometimes it doesn't cross my mind for a full five minutes.

Doug Sanders

Golf is assuredly a mystifying
game. It would seem that if
a person has hit a golf ball
correctly a thousand times,
he should be able to duplicate
the performance at will. But
such is certainly not the case.

Bobby Jones

67

68

The winds were blowing 50 mph and gusting to 70. I hit par 3 with my hat.

Chi Chi Rodriguez

I sure was glad I ran out of holes.
I looked down at my hands and
arms to see if it was me when I
finished with the score.

Don January

70

The truly great things happen
when a genius is alone.
This is true especially among golfers.

J. R. Coulson

One of the nice things about
the Senior Tour is that
we can take a cart and cooler.
If your game is not going well,
you can always have a picnic.

Lee Trevino

71

72

The odds of hitting a duffed shot
increase by the square of the
number of people watching.

Henry Beard
(Mulligan's Laws)

A perfectly straight shot with
a BIG CLUB is a fluke!

Jack Nicklaus

73

74

I never knew what top golf was like
until I turned professional.
Then it was too late.

Steve Melnyk

Golf is deceptively simple and endlessly complicated; it satisfies the soul and frustrates the intellect. It is at the same time rewarding and maddening—and it is without a doubt the greatest game mankind has ever invented.

Arnold Palmer

75

76

I never pray on the golf course.
Actually, the Lord answers my prayers
everywhere except on the course.

Rev. Billy Graham

Thinking instead of acting is the
number-one golf disease.

Sam Snead

77

78

On the golf course, a man may be
the dogged victim of inexorable fate,
be struck down by an appalling stroke
of tragedy, become the hero of
unbelievable melodrama, or the
clown in a side-splitting comedy.

Bobby Jones

There are two things you can
do with your head down—
play golf and pray.

Lee Trevino

79

In golf, humiliations are the
essence of the game.

Alistair Cooke

When you play the game for fun, it's fun. When you play it for a living, it's a game of sorrows.

Gary Player

81

82

Golf is the hardest game in the world.
There's no way you can ever get it.
Just when you think you do, the game
jumps up and puts you into your place.

Ben Crenshaw

Nothing goes down slower
than a golf handicap.

Bobby Nichols

83

84

The ball's got to stop somewhere.
It might as well be
at the bottom of the hole.

Lee Trevino

Golf is an easy game . . .
it's just hard to play.

Unknown

85

You know what they say
about the big hitters . . .
the woods are full of them.

Jimmy Demaret

Happiness is a long walk
with a putter.

Greg Norman

87

88

Nobody asks you how you looked,
just what you shot.

Sam Snead

Golf tips are like aspirin. One may
do you good, but if you swallow
the whole bottle you will be
lucky to survive.

Harvey Penick

89

He enjoys that perfect peace,
that peace beyond all understanding,
which comes at its maximum only
to the man who has given up golf.

P. G. Wodehouse

If you call on God to improve the results of a shot while it is still in motion, you are using 'an outside agency' and subject to appropriate penalties under the rules of golf.

Henry Longhurst

91

92

Competitive golf is played mainly on
a five-and-a-half-inch course,
the space between your ears.

Bobby Jones

If your caddie coaches you on the tee, "Hit it down the left side with a little draw," ignore him. All you do on the tee is try not to hit the caddie.

Jim Murray

93

94

Everybody has two swings . . .
a beautiful practice swing and the
choked-up one with which they hit the
ball. So it wouldn't do either of us a bit
of good to look at your practice swing.

Ed Furgol

The person I fear most in the
last two rounds is myself.

Tom Watson

95

96

I'd give up golf if I didn't have
so many sweaters.

Bob Hope

Golf is like fishing and hunting.
What counts is the companionship
and fellowship of friends, not
what you catch or shoot.

George Archer

97

98

We speak of eyeball-to-eyeball encounters between men great and small. Even more reaching and revealing of character is the eyeball-to-golfball confrontation, whereby our most secret natures are mercilessly tested by a small, round, whitish object with no mind or will but with a very definite life of its own, and with whims perverse and beatific.

John Stewart Martin

I'd like to see the fairways
more narrow. Then everybody
would have to play from
the rough, not just me.

Steve Ballesteros

99

100

Obviously a deer on the fairway
has seen you tee off before and knows
that the safest place to be
when you play
is right down the middle.

Jackie Gleason

Why am I using a new putter?
Because the last one didn't
float too well.

Craig Stadler

101

102

A professional will tell you the amount
of flex you need in the shaft of your
club. The more the flex, the more
strength you will need to break
the thing over your knees.

Stephen Baker

When he gets the ball
into a tough place,
that's when he's most relaxed.
I think it's because
he has so much experience at it.

Don Christopher
(Jack Lemmon's caddie)

103

104

My game is so bad I gotta hire
three caddies . . . one to walk the
left rough, one for the right, and one
for the middle. And the one in the
middle doesn't have much to do.

Dave Hill

You can't lose an old golf ball.

John Willis

Golf is the only sport that a professional
can enjoy playing with his friends.

Chi Chi Rodriguez

Golf is a good walk spoiled.

Mark Twain

108

The fun you get from golf is in
direct ratio to the effort you
don't put into it.

Bob Allen

You've just one problem.
You stand too close to the ball
after you've hit it.

Sam Snead

109

110

The only shots you can be sure of
are those you've had already.

Byron Nelson

If you watch a game, it's fun.
If you play it, it's recreation.
If you work at it, it's golf.

Bob Hope

111

Mulligan: Invented by an Irishman
who wanted to hit one more
twenty-yard grounder.

Jim Bishop

It's nice to have people watching.
They help me find my ball
sometimes.

Jack Nicklaus II

113

114

Golf is 20 percent mechanics and technique. The other 80 percent is philosophy, humor, tragedy, romance, melodrama, companionship, camaraderie, cussedness, and conversation.

Grantland Rice

There are no points for style when it comes to putting. It's getting the ball in the cup that counts.

Brian Swarbrick

115

116

Putts get real difficult the day
they hand out the money.

Lee Trevino

Golf is an ideal diversion, but
ruinous disease.

Bertie Forbes

117

118

Golf is a game where guts and
blind devotion will always net you
absolutely nothing but an ulcer.

Tommy Bolt

I'm hitting the woods just great,
but I'm having a terrible time
getting out of them.

Harry Tofcano

120

A lot of guys who have never choked
have never been
in the position to do so.

Tom Watson

The sum total of the rules
[of etiquette in golf]
is thoughtfulness.

Abe Mitchell

121

122

Golf: a day spent in a round of
strenuous idleness.

William Wordsworth

Relax? How can anybody relax and
play golf? You have to grip the
club don't you?

Ben Hogan

123

124

Golf is a game whose aim is to hit a very small ball into an even smaller hole with weapons singularly ill-designed for the purpose.

Winston Churchill

If you think it's hard to meet new
people, try picking up the
wrong golf ball.

Jack Lemmon

125

126

The older you get the stronger the wind gets . . . and it's always in your face.

Jack Nicklaus

The fundamental problem with golf is that every so often, no matter how lacking you may be in the essential virtues required of a steady player, the odds are that one day you will hit the ball straight, hard, and out of sight. This is the essential frustration of this excruciating sport. For when you've done it once, you make the fundamental error of asking yourself why you can't do this all the time. The answer to this question is simple: the first time was a fluke.

Colin Bowles

127

Eighteen holes of match play will teach
you more about your foe than
nineteen years of dealing
with him across the desk.

Grantland Rice

If you don't take it seriously it's
not fun; if you do take it seriously,
it breaks your heart.

Arnold Daly

Golf is not a wrestle with bogey; it is not a struggle with your mortal foe. It is a physiological, psychological, and moral fight with your self; it is a test of mastery over self; and the ultimate and irreducible element of the game is to determine which of the players is the more worthy combatant.

Arnold Haultain

It took me seventeen years to get
three thousand hits in baseball.
I did it in one afternoon on
the golf course.

Hank Aaron

131

No matter how short the par three,
the drive is never a gimme.

Mulligan's Laws

If the wind is in your face, you swing too hard just to get the ball through it; if the wind is at your back, you swing too hard just to see how far you can get the ball to go.

Mulligan's Laws

133

Putting isn't golf. Greens should be treated almost the same as water hazards: you land on them then add two strokes to your score.

Chi Chi Rodriguez

I still swing the way I used to, but
when I look up the ball is going in
a different direction.

Lee Trevino

135

136

Real golfers go to work to relax.

George Dillon

I'd rather play golf and break even
than work hard
and come out ahead.

Mike Donald

137

138

Many a golfer prefers a golf cart
to a caddy because it cannot count,
criticize, or laugh.

Unknown

An amateur golfer is one who
addresses the ball twice . . .
once before swinging and
once again after swinging.

Unknown

Golf is a game in which the slowest people in the world are those in front of you, and the fastest are those behind.

Unknown

The man who takes up golf to get his mind off his work soon takes up work to get his mind off golf.

Unknown

141

142

It's good sportsmanship to not pick up
lost balls while they are still rolling.

Mark Twain

The most important thing for
golfers of all ages and handicaps is
not that they should play golf
well, but that they should
play it cheerfully.

H. J. Whigham

143

The game can be played in company or alone. Robinson Crusoe on his island, with his man Friday as a caddie, could have realized the golfer's dream of perfect happiness—a fine day, a good course, and a clear green.

Henry E. Howland

Golf: A game in which you claim
the privileges of age, and retain
the playthings of childhood.

Samuel Johnson

145

146

It is almost impossible to remember
how tragic a place the world is
when one is playing golf.

Robert Lynd

It is this constant and undying
hope for improvement
that makes golf so
exquisitely worth the playing.

Bernard Darwin

147

148

Golf is a compromise between what your ego wants you to do, what experience tells you to do, and what your nerves will let you do.

Bruce Crampton

The only way of really finding out
a man's true character is
to play golf with him.

P. G. Wodehouse

149

Golf appeals to the idiot in us and the child. Just how childlike golf players become is proven by their frequent inability to count past five.

John Updike

Golf swings are like snowflakes.
There are no two exactly alike.

Peter Jacobsen

151

152

Golfers as a rule are an exceptionally
honest race of men, but uncertain
arithmetic is occasionally
encountered on the green.

Henry E. Howland

My sole ambition in the game is to
do well enough to give it up.

David Feherty

153

154

The only reason I played golf was so I could afford to hunt and fish.

Sam Snead

Getting in a water hazard is like
being in a plane crash—
the result is final.
Landing in a bunker is similar to
an automobile accident—
there is a chance of recovery.

Bobby Jones

155

156

The cardinal error which players
commit today when they practice is to
nudge each shot into a perfect lie.

Gene Sarazen

Through years of experience, I
have found that air offers less
resistance than dirt.

Jack Nicklaus

157

158

There are no secrets to golf. The secret of success is practice, constant but intelligent practice.

Ernest Jones

Baseball reveals character;
golf exposes it.

Ernie Banks

159

Additional copies of this book are available
from your local bookstore.

Also available from Honor Books:

God's Little Instruction Book
The Golfer's Tee Time Devotional

If you have enjoyed this book, or if it has
impacted your life, we would like to hear from you.
Please contact us at:

Honor Books
Department E
P.O. Box 55388
Tulsa, Oklahoma 74137
Or by e-mail at info@honorbooks.com